BANE

By

Lyn Murray

Golden Panda Publishing

USA

Presented by

Golden Panda Publishing

Copyright ® 2015

ISBN-13: 978-1512257700

ISBN-10: 1512257702

Lyn Murray – All Rights Reserved

Golden Panda Publishing, USA

Copyrighted ® Material

This publication may not be reproduced in whole or in part, stored in a retrieval system, or transmitted in any form, by any means electronic, mechanical, printing, photocopying, recording, etc.; without written consent of the author or publisher, except for the inclusion of brief quotations in a review.

"Wake up!"

It's not the lies you recognize that take you down – it's the smiling face with a hidden knife that **stabs** you in the back!"

Lyn Murray

Preface

Loose and free – that's how we like to think of ourselves living our lives. *Freedom!* In total control – living the good life in the good ole U.S.A. . . . but are we just fooling ourselves into an early grave?

You'd think our hard earned tax dollars would help do more than pave our streets and keep the infrastructure clicking – you'd think the politicians we elect to office (who promise to take care of us) would do the job we hired them to do instead of making promises they intend to break once they're in office.

You'd think!

It's a sad fact that Americans are being sold down the *muddy* River of No Return on the Good Ship *GREED!*

Another *great* <u>Anthological Novella</u> *by author Lyn Murray* – **Bane** is a fictional allegory based on real things that are going on right now in America that are making us sick and taking our lives – while the politicians stuff their pockets with blood money.

Your blood – Your money!

The characters in this book are based on *real people* (whose names have been changed to protect their privacy) – who got an unexpected wake-up call that nearly cost them their lives. While the contents seem too fantastic to be real – I assure you – reality put this book together with a message for you to Wake Up! You don't live in the world you think you do – and this is NOT Disneyland.

The Walking Dead are among us – *<u>and they are YOU</u>*!

Lyn's VIMEO Video

Monsanto – You're Invited!

&

Lyn Murray's YouTube

GMO Humans – Hugens!

TIPS

***for* reading Lyn's Anthologies:**

When you get to the title story – read it all the way through (without clicking any links) so you don't lose the story.

After you've read **Bane** through – THEN – go back and open each link for a whole new experience!

Table of Contents

Presented by 3

"Wake up!" 7

Preface 9

Lyn's VIMEO Video 11

Lyn Murray's YouTube 11

TIPS 13

BANE 17

   Chapter 1 17

   Chapter 2 21

   Chapter 3 55

   Chapter 4 - Tomorrow 79

     The Monsanto Legacy? 103

   Chapter 5 - A Dark eMail 107

Addendum 121

    Ultimate Killing Machine 121

You're Not Fat - You're Toxic 136

"The Most Evil Corporation" 139

NODS 175

For Sushi Lovers Everywhere! 176

    "You Are What You Eat" 177

    Now you know! 183

Legal Stuff 185

About the Author 187

Lyn's Other Books 191

Thank You! 193

Our Intrepid Duo - *Yesterday* 195

The Salvation Army 199

BANE

Chapter 1

What's *Hump Day* Between Friends

Every Wednesday – like clockwork – Alice, Denise, Gale and Francis would meet like those popular TV friends in "Sex and the City" at their favorite restaurant and bar, indulge in a few drinks, talk about their week and the week ahead, and about the men in their lives.

They overlooked Alice's temper flares when the waiter delivered the wrong drink, Gale's bizarre laugh that more nearly resembled a braying Jack Ass, Francis' low-cut frocks befitting the highest paid prostitute money could buy, and even tolerated Denise's pension for and obsession with Conspiracy Theories – not because they particularly enjoyed each other's quirks – that's just what friends do. You overlook shit and move on.

However, this evening began even quirkier than usual with Denise's refusal to eat anything on the menu. The ensuing conversation when something like this:

The Girls/Left to Right:

Denise, Alice, Gale & Francis

Chapter 2

Conspiracy Theory Central

Gale asked, "Now what is it? You've looked through the menu four times?"

"I can't find anything to eat."

Denise's companions briefly glanced at each other, then back to her.

Francis cackled, "Can't find anything to eat? The menu is full of food. Pick something!"

"Nothing natural. I can't find anything natural. It's all processed." Denise said, flipping through the menu again from front to back.

Alice chimed in, "Turn to the back. Pick something from the "Garden Fresh" section. A nice salad, maybe?"

"I looked at that. . . . *I don't think so.*"

"For crying out loud, Denise," Gale chirped, "how about a nice shrimp salad – you love shrimp!"

"Can't – Corexit!"

"What?!" Alice barked, "Corexit?! What the fuck is Corexit?"

Denise pulled down her glasses, looking over the tops to glare at Gale while attempting to answer her unwitting question, "Corexit?

Corexit? You don't know what Corexit is? It's that shit they poured in the Gulf to try and break up the BP Deepwater Horizon oil spill in 2010 – *that was still going strong in 2013. Surely you remember it – it was only all over the news, until the government shut the stream of information down!*

That oil spill that pretty much killed the Gulf and every living thing in it – not to mention destroying the Gulf Stream.

It's going to take marine life a hundred or more years to recover – *if then!*

Of course – *then . . . !*"

"You had to ask," Gale said, "here it comes . . . "

British Petroleum Deepwater Oil Spill

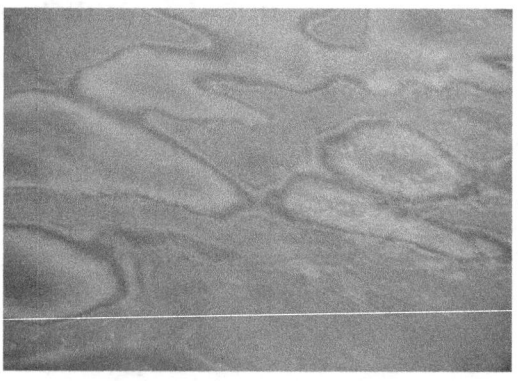

Oil in the Gulf

Suffering Oil Covered Wildlife

**BP Deepwater Oil Spill
Gulf of Mexico**

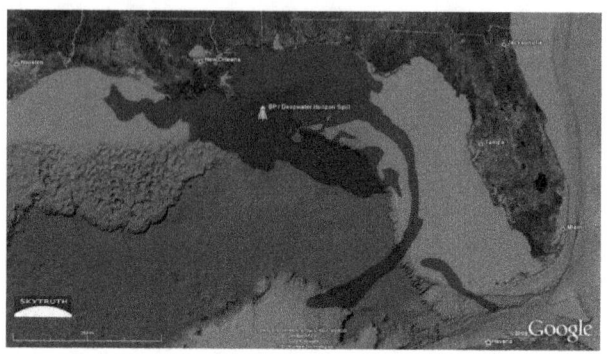

Immediate Area Affected

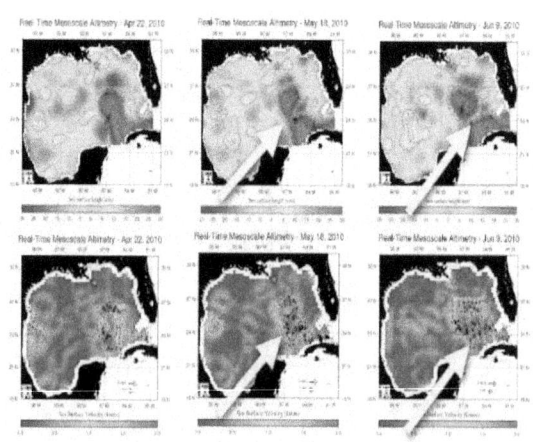

Arial Shots of Damaged Gulf Stream Loop

"Factual satellite images in the past several weeks are showing that the Gulf Loop Current is broken and may cease to function entirely! This will result in massive climate change and possibly an ice age for Europe! Major trouble brewing?? More freakish weather on its way??"

◊◊◊

"*Scoff if you must,* but that spill and Corexit has killed the Gulf of Mexico – thousands of various types of marine life from Dolphins to Turtles (and everything in between) have died (and are dying still) – some marine life specific to the area will not be seen again in your lifetime. Maybe never! There have even been human causalities (but the powers that be try to keep a lid on those losses)!

Then there's the Gulf Stream. *Totally fucked up!* If you're wondering about all the recent strange weather – look no further!

Then Fukushima in 2014 . . .!"

(Alice) "For God's sake!"

"Well?! Do you want to eat chemical and nuclear waste?"

(Gale) "OMG!" (Oh My God!)

"Well – do you?"

(Francis) "Then, have a salad."

"What?"

Francis repeated, "Eat a nice salad. You love Caesar Salad."

"Yes, I do – or did, but practically everything salad based is now GMO."

(Alice) "OK – I'll bite. What is GMO?"

Denise put the menu down and folded her hands on top of it while looking across the table at her companions, first one – then another. "I cannot believe I hang out with you people! Where have you been? Do any of you ever seek out alternative news from reliable sources like the <u>Drudge Report</u> – OR – <u>The Huffington Post</u>? "Cause you're not gonna get the truth from mainstream news sources like Fox and CNN! They're too busy cramming the controlling whims of <u>Constitution Hating/Government Takeover</u>

[False Flag](#) political charlatans down our [Sheeple](#) gullets.

I guess you also believe the [Boston Bombing](#) happened the way they said?! Honestly – do the lot of you only read romance novels – (PFH/porn for housewives)?"

(Gale) "Hey – I watch Nova!"

They all laughed.

Francis held up her hand, "I watch the History Channel."

Alice pointed to herself, "Animal Planet!"

"For God's sake," Denise said, "I'm being serious, here . . ."

As if choreographed, they all said, *"I know!"*

"I'm serious! GMO?! None of you know about GMO foods? Monsanto? Any of you ever hear of Monsanto? Bayer – perhaps?"

(Alice) "Don't they make pesticides?"

Denise snapped her fingers and pointed to Alice, "Give the woman a prize! Yes, Alice – and the rest of you – Monsanto makes pesticides, which they feed to you by way of GMO's – Genetically Modified Foods."

Longing for a nice quiet, relaxing evening out, but settling in for another of Denise's tirades, Gale said, waving her hand in the air trying to flag down a waiter, "Can we order a drink before I lose the will to live?"

When a nice looking young man in his mid-twenties reached their table to take her order, Gale ordered everyone's usual before returning her attention to the conversation. "OK – since you're going to *anyway* . . . tell us about Monsanto and GMO foods."

Another longing surfaced –

(Francis) "Can we eat first? I may not want to eat by the time she's through trashing everything on the menu."

"Well," Denise snapped, "maybe you won't, but you'll still be alive to gripe about me having ruined your appetite!"

(Gale) "Last week – it was <u>Chem Trails.</u> *Now this!*"

Denise snarled, "Will you just shut up and listen? You might learn something. I don't

know (all this time) obviously I've been talking to hear myself rattle."

(Alice) "Fine – but I'm ordering. If my food's going to kill me – at least I'll die with a full belly," she said.

"Have it your way, but the food you're about to eat is *septic* – poisoned! Practically all food is GMO now, and they're engineered with enzymes that are supposed to kill insects by corrupting their DNA, and eat them from the inside out – enzymes that survive the food preparation process that are now eating you from the inside out. But you go ahead . . . eat up. *Bon Appétit!*"

"What?" Alice said, first looking over her menu – then folding and putting it down. "*Enzymes?* Eating us from the inside? What the hell are you saying?"

The others folded their menus.

(Francis) "Is this a joke?"

"I couldn't be more serious," Denise said, "it's the scariest of truths!"

Pictures of parasitic infestation throughout the human body began to flash through their minds.

"OMG! I think I'm going to throw up." Alice gurgled.

"Wait a minute," Gale said, "I thought the FDA (Food and Drug Administration had to approve all food and food processes? They're supposed to be protecting us against bad players! *Aren't they?*"

"Are they? It doesn't just stop with food – FDA also governs

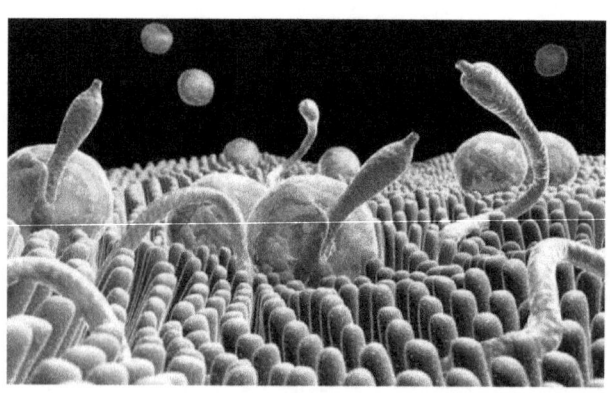

(or is supposed to govern) pharmaceuticals – but how many class action lawsuits involving bad drugs have you seen on TV lately?

And Cancer . . . don't get me started about Cancer treatment – that's **designed to kill you slowly . . . not cure.** You cannot destroy your immune system . . . then expect it to save you! But that's what Chemo Therapy and the *old standby* Radiation does! Do you know that most cancer survivors end up with Leukemia?"

They all shook their heads, *no*.

"Do you know why?"

Again they shook their heads, *no*.

"Because Chemo and Radiation destroys the bone marrow! It's a fact you won't read in Physician's Weekly magazine or on the Modern Medicine Network, I promise you! 75% (it's believed that number is actually much higher, ranging somewhere in the 90 percentile) of all physicians queried, reported they would ***never*** have Chemo and conventional cancer therapy. Not for themselves. Not for anyone they love! What does that tell you? But the FDA – boy, they're backing conventional cancer therapy 100%! You bet they are! Why? Because from *diagnosis to grave* a cancer patient is worth about ***a million bucks***! That's why!"

(Francis) "I don't understand? If the FDA isn't protecting us — then who are they protecting?"

Denise pulled down even farther the glasses on the bridge of her nose before saying, *"Really? You have to ask?"*

(Alice) "You're insane! That's impossible! How can you even suggest that our legislators would stand for such collusion?"

"I cannot believe that we've been friends for eight years — and you don't know the answer to that," Denise said.

"They're part of it — they voted it in."

(Gale) "Why? What possible motive could they have? *You're nuts!*"

(Alice) "That's what I've been

trying to tell all of you – she's nuts!"

(Denise) "Kickbacks – anyone ever hear of those?"

(Gale) "They eat the same food as the rest of us!"

"Do they?" Denise said. ". . . Ever wonder why the White House refuses to eat store-bought *anything* and insists own growing their on veggies, etc. . . . ?"

"They do?" Francis asked.

"You bet they do! Long before Obama took office – Michelle Obama made it quite clear that they only ate *organic foods* – including meat from cattle that have been raised to slaughter on **pesticide-free grains.** In other words – no GMOs."

(Francis) "Seriously?"

(Denise) "Seriously!"

"In fact – when they moved into the White House – they brought their on chef! And they only buy meat from an organic farmer . . . 150 miles away! What does that tell you?"

(Gale) "No shit?"

(Denise) "No shit! In a

Huffington Post blog by reporter David Kirby on May 10, 2015 – when asking Michelle Obama's Secretary, "If the sourcing of animal products was any different for food prepared for the First Family, food offered at special events and food served in the White House cafeteria?"

Stating that, "These seemed like reasonable questions to me." Who told Mrs. Obama's office that he did not need specifics on the names or even locations of farms and companies that produce the White House's food, in recognition of security concerns. *But they did not wish to comment:*

"I'm afraid we're not going to be able to address your questions at this time," wrote Katie McCormick

Lelyveld, Mrs. Obama's Press Secretary.

At first Kirby was surprised and a bit bemused, saying, "After all, is it really a state secret whether the Obama family prefers Tyson "Evencook Chicken Breasts" to pasture-raised birds from, say, Joel Salatin's Polyface Farm in Swoop, VA, 150 miles away?"

But after thinking about it, he said that he couldn't really blame them for not wanting to comment. "In fact," he said, "I can sympathize. The topic is *that* volcanic."

Alice rubbed her midriff. "You know, come to think of it, I haven't been feeling well lately. Not after that outing at Nancy's bridal shower last week."

"Something you ate?" asked Gale.

"I don't know? Nobody else seemed bothered by the menu . . ." Alice said.

(Denise) "Not everyone is affected by GMO the same way – OR – at the same time; but all of us are being affected – *genetically changed*. Sooner than later – it will compromise the health of everything that consumes it."

Alice picked up her menu, saying, "I think I'll just have soup – maybe a good broth type soup – and green tea. Maybe salad? How about you, Francis?"

"I think I'll try a salad, but instead of my usual dressing I'll just have vinegar and oil."

"Me too," Gale said, looking over at Denise. "How about you?"

"Green tea for me – if it's organic." And after successfully hailing the waiter, they ordered, and tried to divert Denise's persistent, twisted tunnel vision toward a more pleasant topic.

(Gale) "Tell us about Nancy's bridal shower. I bet it was lavish, wasn't it?"

(Alice) "You know it was! Her parents don't know another approach – *to anything!*

It was held at their place in the Hamptons and catered by none other than the world- renowned *Lenôtre of Paris.*"

Her companions chimed together, "You're kidding?!"

"No!"

(Denise) *More thinking to herself than anything, she mumbled,* "It couldn't have been their food – Europeans don't eat GMOs. They're banned from most European countries."

But Francis heard the comment, and asked, "Is that right?!"

(Denise) "You bet it is! The European Union (EU) may have the most stringent GMO regulations in the world. All GMOs (along with irradiated food) are considered *"new food"* and are subject to extensive, case-by-case, science-based food evaluation by the European Food Safety Authority (EFSA). The EFSA reports to the European Commission, which then drafts proposals for granting or refusing authorization. Each proposal is submitted to the Section on GM Food and Feed of the Standing Committee on the Food Chain and Animal Health. If accepted, it is either adopted by the EC or passed on to the Council of Agricultural Ministers. The Council has three months to reach a qualified majority for or against the proposal. If no majority is reached, the proposal is passed back to the EC, which then adopts the proposal.

As of September 2014, 49 GMOs, consisting of eight GM cottons, 28 GM maizes, three GM oilseed rapes, seven GM soybeans, one GM sugar beet, one GM bacterial biomass, and one GM yeast biomass have been authorized.

There is a safeguard clause that Member States may invoke to temporarily restrict or prohibit the use and/or sale of a GMO within their territory if they have justifiable reasons to consider that the approved GMO constitutes a risk to human health or the environment. The EC is obliged to investigate these cases and either overturn the original registrations or ask the country to withdraw its temporary restriction. By 2012, seven countries had submitted safeguard clauses. The EC investigated and rejected those from six countries, ("...the scientific evidence currently available did not invalidate the original risk assessments for the products in question..."), and one (the UK) withdrew.

France adopted the EU laws on growing GMOs in 2007 and were fined €10 million by the European Court of Justice for the six-year delay in implementing the laws. In February 2008 the French government used the safeguard clause to ban the cultivation of MON 810 after Senator Jean-François Le Grand, chairman of a committee set up to evaluate biotechnology, said there were "serious doubts" about the safety of the product. Twelve scientists and two economists on the committee accused Le Grand of misrepresenting the report and say they did not have "serious doubts" although questions remained concerning the impact of Bt-maize on health and the environment.

The French government submitted a number of studies to back up its claim to the EU. These were given to the EFSA who concluded that there was no new evidence to undermine the previous safety findings and considered the decision "scientifically unfounded".

The [High Council for Biotechnology](#) Subcommittee dealing with economic, ethical and social aspects recommended an additional "GMO-free" label for anything containing less than 0.1% GMO, which is due to come in late 2010.

So – it had to have been something else that made you queasy."

Francis chuckled, "She's a virtual encyclopedia, – I tell you!"

Denise smirked, "What else did you eat or drink, Alice?"

As Alice thought about that – their meals were delivered to the table.

Dribbling her salad with Vinegar and Oil, Alice said, "Nancy and I ate breakfast at a local fast food joint..."

(Denise) "That's probably what did it. What did you have?"

"I can't really remember. Some kind of breakfast sausage thingy, I think."

(Denise) "Hum? But you didn't begin to feel bad until later in the day?"

"Right. Haven't felt good since. Stomach's been awfully upset."

(Denise) "Hum. Well . . . try to eat your salad and forget all this talk about GMOs for now."

(Alice) "I couldn't agree more! Let's just enjoy our visit and catch up on gossip!"

(Gale) "Absolutely! You've probably just got a touch of the virus. *You'll be fine!*" As the four of them set about trying to forget Denise's tirade concerning the poison food supply – somehow the conversation veered toward our prehistoric "Electoral College" and the 2007 HBO documentary: **Hacking America**, created by producers' Robert Carrillo Cohen, Russell Michaels and Simon Ardizzone, Sarah Teale & Sian Edwards, that took over three years to film, focusing on the *joke* of **Black Box Voting** in America that boiled down to:

Whomever the Powers that Be Are" – they will see the person elected that they **want** elected – and individual votes by Patriotic America has "little" *if anything* to do with it! The prime example of that being the presidential election of 2000 between George Bush and Al Gore – where millions of *voting* Americans watched the "election results map" on CNN and Fox News <u>miraculously and instantaneously</u> switch from Blue to Red . . . declaring Bush/Cheney the winners!

This groundbreaking documentary was so well done that in 2007 it was nominated for an <u>Emmy Award</u> for Outstanding Long Form Investigative Journalism.

As these **"tour de force"** *friends settled into a more relaxed mode,* nothing was sacred, including their co-workers' dirtiest laundry, *OR* how cute tonight's Latino pianist was.

However, although she tried, Alice could not get comfortable and continued to rub her midriff, making the occasional comment about not feeling quite well, until toward the end of their meal she grabbed her stomach screaming – before doubling over in pain and tumbling to the floor – as her friends looked on in horror.

Chapter 3

The Nightmare Within

With Alice's companions rushing to her side – Denise dialed 911 …

"911 – what is your emergency?"

"My friend just grabbed her stomach screaming and passed out in the floor of the restaurant we're dining at."

"Is your friend pregnant?"

"No. Not that I know of."

"What is your location?"

"We are at Belininns' Restaurant and Bar on Wellington Blvd."

"Don't hang up. Stay on the phone."

There was background noise as the dispatcher routed the EMS crew before she returned to Denise, asking, "Is your friend conscious?"

Unable to see Alice, Denise shouted over the crowd to anyone who would answer, "Is she conscious?" "Francis, Gale – is Alice conscious?"

A familiar voice responded. "Not really," Francis replied. "She's in and out of consciousness."

Denise returned to the EMS dispatcher. "No, she is not conscious."

(Dispatcher) "Is she breathing?"

(Denise) "Francis – is she breathing?"

(Francis) "Yes. It's labored, but she's breathing."

(Denise) "Yes, she's breathing."

(Dispatcher) "Keep her comfortable but do not try to move her."

(Denise) "Francis – don't let anyone move her! Keep her comfortable, *but don't move her!*"

(Dispatcher) "What is your friend's age and name, and can you briefly tell me what happened?"

(Denise) "Alice Westland. Twenty-four. I don't know – we were eating. She had been complaining of an upset stomach. Rubbing her midriff. Toward the end of her salad – she grabbed her stomach screaming and passed out in the floor."

(Dispatcher) "Did she vomit?"

(Denise) "No."

(Dispatcher) "Is she blue?"

(Denise) "Francis – is Alice blue?"

(Francis) "No. She has good coloration. Lips are pink. Nail beds are pink. She looks normal – except she's passed out."

(Denise) "No vomit, Francis?"

(Francis) "No! Mouth and throat appear to be clear. *No convulsions.* She's not biting her tongue. She's not doing anything – she's out cold! Her heart is beating – pulse seems a little fast but . . . "

(Denise) "How soon will EMS get here?"

(Dispatcher) "They are en route. You are not far from their point of origin. You should begin to hear the siren shortly."

(Denise) "Yes, yes – I think I hear them."

(Dispatcher) "Stay on the line. Don't hang up!"

(Denise) "I won't. Yes, yes – they're here. I see the lights flashing outside. They're here!"

(Dispatcher) "Stay on the line."

(Denise) "Yes, yes, I'm here."

(Dispatcher) "What is your name and relationship to Alice?"

(Denise) "Denise Sheppard, I'm Denise Sheppard her friend for the past eight years."

(Dispatcher) "Your address and phone number, Ms. Sheppard?"

(Denise) "2108 Collins Ave., number 421. The Breckenridge Estate Townhomes – off Wesleyan."

(Dispatcher) "EMS has confirmed their arrival. They'll take over now. You're in good hands."

(Denise) "Yes. They're here. Thank you. Thank you so much."

(Dispatcher) "You're very welcome. Goodbye now."

(Denise) "Thank you. Bye."

While the EMS crew did their thing – Denise paid the tab and collected Alice's belongings as she and the others prepared to follow the ambulance to the hospital.

As the others saw Alice loaded on the stretcher, Francis headed to the front of the restaurant to have the valet bring the car around so it would be ready to go when the ambulance left.

Once in route to the hospital their talk was centered around Alice and her strange experience at Nancy's shower, with Gale and Francis showing a little more interest and respect for Denise's knowledge of GMO foods.

Little did they know – their respect for Denise's knowledge of such matters was about to increase exponentially after the ER doctor's examination and revelation as to the cause of her sudden collapse.

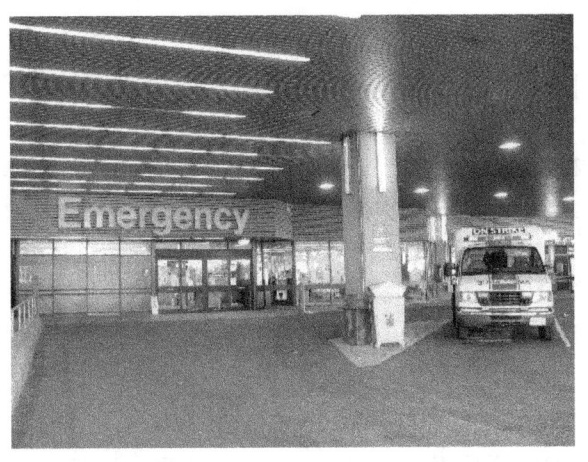

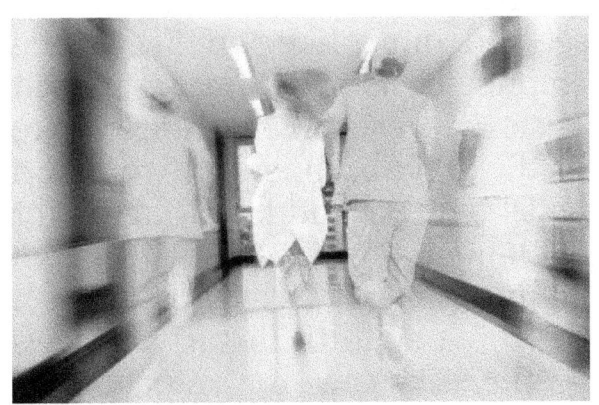

After parking in the hospital's parking garage, they made their way to the E.R., stopping by the receptionist's desk to check Alice in – and all that entails, while establishing themselves as "persons of interest", with Denise telling a blatant lie – that she was Alice's sister (knowing that medical personnel wouldn't talk to anyone but family); then taking a a seat in the waiting room . . . they waited.

After an hour or so (an hour that seemed more like ten, with total combined hours from restaurant crisis to present being somewhere in the neighborhood of two and a half hours) a middle- aged doctor of about fifty emerged from behind sterile locked doors with the first round of disturbing news – the first in a long line of unsettling facts about their friend's health.

"Which one of you is the sister?" he asked.

Denise stepped up. "I am." She put out her hand to shake his. "I'm Denise. How is she?"

Shaking her hand, he motioned for her and her companions to be seated. Taking the seat beside Denise, he began, "Your sister is suffering from a Leaky Gut. Probably the worst that I've seen."

Knowing full well what that was, Denise simply replied, "Really?"

"She's had this condition for quite some time. Has she been complaining of stomach issues?"

"Not really. Only tonight. She did mention that it seemed to begin after eating at a fast food joint in the Hamptons last week."

"I assure you the severity of her condition began much earlier than last week. In my professional opinion, this has been going on for years. Like so many, she probably discounted any discomfort, marking it down as merely being something she ate, and kept ignoring it until her poor body just couldn't take any more. Last week (and tonight) was "the straw that broke the camel's back" so to speak. Forgive me, but frankly – it's a wonder she's still alive! She must have a strong constitution!"

"She does. It's that bad? Really?"

"Your sister has the worst perforated gut that I have ever seen – in someone who is still living."

"She will be all right, though? She's going to be all right?"

"I'm doing my best. There is a lot of damage . . . not only to her intestines, but throughout her body. The organisms and bacteria that escaped her intestines is pervasive throughout, leaving widespread infection. She will require immediate surgery. Her intestines must be removed. I'm sorry to have to say this, but if she lives, she will wear a Colostomy Bag for the remainder of her life. More about that later, right now I'm trying to save her liver. It is so damaged and full of holes. Pustuels have formed inside and out. Her kidneys are in the same shape, and practically non-functioning. Right now, I'm just trying to get her stabilized enough to operate."

Their faces went white.

"I'm sorry to have to ask, but – does she have a living will?"

(Gale) "My god! You don't expect her to make it, do you?"

"I'm doing my best – but you have to understand . . . she's in bad shape. The next twelve hours are crucial."

Francis began to cry.

Denise suddenly stood up. "It's the contaminated food supply, isn't it? It's that damn unregulated GMO food the FDA has allowed into our food supply, isn't it?!" she said, turning to the doctor, reiterating, "Isn't it?!"

"There is mounting evidence to support that, yes. There is still much that we don't understand, but Leaky Gut Syndrome is now a very common condition affecting a high percentage of the population today.

The medical profession has no protocol to diagnose leaky gut syndrome, nor do they (for the most part) readily acknowledge that it even exists. As a result, many people go undiagnosed and are unaware that they may suffer from a leaky gut. But pretty much every chronic degenerative disorder stems from a leaky gut from arthritis, and digestive problems to ME, MS, Chronic Fatigue Syndrome, Irritable Bowel Syndrome (IBS), Fibromyalgia, and neurological disorders to name a few. "

(Denise) "Fuck!" she said turning to her companions, "I told you. I tried to tell you! You don't listen – none of you listen! *Nobody listens!*"

Turning back to the doctor, she continued her rant, ending it with, "You have to save her! Do whatever you must, but save her! I don't know if she has a living will, any kind of will – but she would want to live! She's only twenty-four. Her whole life is ahead of her." Grabbing the doctor's arm, she screamed, "You have to save her!"

The doctor took her hand, "I'm doing everything I can. I've called in a specialist to assist me with tonight's surgery. I'm trying to get her stabilized. If I can get her stabilized, then she has a good chance of surviving. If I can get her stabilized."

(Francis) "And if you can't?"

"She will not survive the night."

(Gale) "My god!"

"If I can get her to surgery there is a good chance that she will survive. She will not be the same ever again. There will be major lifestyle changes. And more surgeries down the road. But if I can stabilize her and get her into surgery – she has a good chance of surviving, and with proper care she can expect to have a fairly normal life. Relatively speaking. If I can get her to surgery and repair what damage I can – now. This can't wait, it must be done now. She has a little better than a 50/50 chance."

(Denise) "My god! Just 50/50?! That's it?"

"I'm afraid so. She has suffered tremendous internal damage. The infection alone would have already killed most people. If I can address the infection and get her white count under control and if I'm able to repair the damage   . . .," he paused.   "Let's just focus on tonight. If we can get her through the night – the following twenty-four hours are promising. I have to get back to her, but I will keep you posted on her progress." Again he paused, "Will you be all right?"

(Denise) "I have to be, don't I? We all do." As the doctor turned to leave, Denise took his hand, 'Please – don't let her die!"

Squeezing her hand, he nodded and smiled his understanding and disappeared through those ever present sterile doors – leaving them alone with their *worst* nightmares.

It would be a long night filled with uncertainties, revelations and changed lives. When the sun rose, their friend would still be clinging to life. All thoughts of the carefree life they once embraced would have vanished with each passing hour, leaving them to face an uncertain world with a scary future, *not of their choosing.*

Questions about how this was allowed to happen, of why our food supply wasn't being protected, was utmost in their thoughts – and they knew they had to warn people on a massive scale. People had to know, they had to understand that their on government, the very politicians that had been elected to office were in bed with the "movers and shakers" of the world, and that profit over protection was the driving force behind all decisions that were being made for every living thing on Earth.

People had to know! They had to know now!

"Organic," Denise said, "It's the

only way! Or food we grow ourselves. *We can't trust anyone.*"

(Gale) "Do as the Obama's do, huh?"

(Francis) "If we want to live!"

(Denise) "Exactly!"

Francis searched her purse for change for the vending machine. "Coffee anyone?"

Denise and Gale both answered, "Yes – black. No cream!" They passed on the cinnamon roll as well because they're sweetened with "high fructose corn syrup" which is made from GMO corn, just as most processed foods are!"

(Gale) "I'm going to miss those. I used to love a good cinnamon roll with my coffee in the morning."

(Denise) "You'll just have to learn to make your own using all natural Non-GMO ingredients. That's all. You can do it. You have too. We all do. Everyone does! Until we can convince government officials that we're not going to buy their poisons."

(Francis) "That's it. If we stop buying their poison – they'll be forced to start producing safe foods or face bankruptcy!"

(Denise) "Wouldn't hurt my feelings if they all went out of business!"

(Gale) "Change starts with one person. Alice is our one person. We have to share her story with others."

(Francis) "Facebook! Post Alice's story everywhere. Start a movement and don't let up until the food industry is forced to change the way they grow and process our food. People aren't stupid. They will eventualy listen. *They must* – their lives and the lives of everyone they love are at stake."

(Gale) "If things don't change – we will all die."

(Denise) "Well, that's what <u>Agenda 21</u> is all about! . . . Depopulate the world. It's spelled out in the <u>Georgia Guidestones</u> – for those who can pull their respective heads out of their respective asses. And one of the best ways to achieve their goal is to <u>weaponize our food through GMOs</u>!"

(Francis) "I can't do this right now, Denise. *I can't!* I know that you have something to tell us that's important to our safety and survival – but I just can't hear it right now. Too much going on. *Agenda 21?* Please – save that for another day. Tell us tomorrow? Okay?"

(Denise) "All right. Okay. Tomorrow."

Chapter 4
Tomorrow

As the girls continue their efforts to digest everything that's happened within the past 24 hours – they open an email from Denise with one word in the subject line: *Tomorrow*.

Without having to look – they knew what it meant: that Tomorrow had arrived and with it more "new" information they were dreading learning.

It began before you were born – before any of us were born. Monsanto has always been evil and began the process of killing us back in the early 1900s.

Founded in 1901 by <u>John Francis Queeny</u>, Monsanto initially produced food additives like saccharin and vanillin, expanded into industrial chemicals like sulfuric acid and PCBs in the 1920s, and by the 1940s was a major producer of plastics, including polystyrene and synthetic fibers. Notable achievements by Monsanto and its scientists as a chemical company included breakthrough research on catalytic asymmetric hydrogenation and being the first company to mass-produce light emitting diodes (LEDs). The company also formerly manufactured controversial products such as the insecticide DDT, PCBs, Agent Orange, and recombinant bovine somatotropin (a.k.a. bovine growth hormone).

Let's start with . . .
The Baker's Dirty Dozen:

#1 —

Saccharin

Did you know Monsanto got started because of an artificial sweetener? John Francisco Queeny founded Monsanto Chemical Works in St. Louis, Missouri with the goal of producing saccharin for Coca-Cola. In stark contrast to its sweet beginnings, studies performed during the early 1970s,* including a study by the National Cancer Institute in 1980, showed that saccharin caused cancer in test rats and mice.

After mounting pressure from consumers, the Calorie Control Council, and manufacturers of artificial sweeteners and diet sodas, along with additional studies (several conducted by the sugar and sweetener industry) that reported flaws in the 1970s studies, saccharin was delisted from the NIH's Carcinogen List. A variety of letters from scientists advised against delisting; the official document includes the following wording to this day: "although it is impossible to absolutely conclude that it poses no threat to human health, sodium saccharin is not reasonably anticipated to be a human carcinogen under conditions of general usage as an artificial sweetener." (*Read the Chemical Heritage Foundation's History of Saccharin here.)

#2 –
PCBs

During the early 1920s, Monsanto began expanding their chemical production into polychlorinated biphenyls (PCBs) to produce coolant fluids for electrical transformers, capacitors, and electric motors. Fifty years later, toxicity tests began reporting serious health effects from PCBs in laboratory rats exposed to the chemical.

After another decade of studies, the truth could no longer be contained: the U.S. Environmental Protection Agency (EPA) published a report citing PCBs as the cause of cancer in animals, with additional evidence that they can cause cancer in humans. Additional peer-reviewed health studies showed a causal link between exposure to PCBs and non-Hodgkin Lymphoma, a frequently fatal form of cancer.

In 1979, the United States Congress recognized PCBs as a significant environmental toxin and persistent organic pollutant, and banned its production in the U.S. By then Monsanto already had manufacturing plants abroad, so they weren't entirely stopped until the Stockholm Convention on Persistent Organic Pollutants banned PCBs globally in 2001.

And that's when Monsanto's duplicity was uncovered: internal company memos from 1956 surfaced, proving that Monsanto had known about dangers of PCBs from early on.

In 2003, Monsanto paid out over $600 million to residents of Anniston, Alabama, who experienced severe health problems including liver disease, neurological disorders and cancer after being exposed to PCBs — more than double the payoff that was awarded in the case against Pacific Gas & Electric made famous by the movie "Erin Brockovich."

And yet the damage persists: nearly 30 years after PCBs have been banned from the U.S., they are still showing up in the blood of pregnant women, as reported in a 2011 study by the University of California San Francisco; while other studies are indicating a parallel between PCBs and autism.

#3 – Polystyrene

In 1941, Monsanto began focusing on plastics and synthetic polystyrene, which is still widely used in food packaging and ranked 5th in the EPA's 1980s listing of chemicals whose production generates the most total hazardous waste.

#4 – Atom bomb and Nuclear Weapons

Shortly after acquiring Thomas and Hochwalt Laboratories,

Monsanto turned this division into their Central Research Department. Between 1943 to 1945, this department coordinated key production efforts of the Manhattan Project—including plutonium purification and production and, as part of the Manhattan Project's Dayton Project, techniques to refine chemicals used as triggers for atomic weapons (an era of U.S. history that sadly included the deadliest industrial accident).

**#5 –
DDT**

In 1944, Monsanto became one of the first manufacturers of the insecticide DDT to combat malaria-transmitting mosquitoes. Despite decades of Monsanto propaganda insisting that DDT was safe, the true effects of DDT's toxicity were at last confirmed through outside research and in 1972, DDT was banned throughout the U.S.

#6 –
Dioxin

In 1945, Monsanto began promoting the use of chemical pesticides in agriculture with the manufacture of the herbicide 2,4,5-T (one of the precursors to Agent Orange), containing dioxin. Dioxins are a group of chemically-related compounds that since become known as one of the "Dirty Dozen" — persistent environmental pollutants that accumulate in the food chain, mainly in the fatty tissue of animals. In the decades since it was first developed, Monsanto has been accused of covering up or failing to report dioxin contamination in a wide range of its products.

#7 –
Agent Orange

During the early 1960s, Monsanto was one of the two primary manufacturers of Agent Orange, an herbicide / defoliant used for chemical warfare during the Vietnam War. Except Monsanto's formula had dioxin levels many times higher than the Agent Orange produced by Dow Chemicals, the other manufacturer (which is why Monsanto was the key defendant in the lawsuit brought by Vietnam War veterans in the United States).

(Pictured at left, Anh and Trang Nhan, with their father, when they first arrived at the Hoi An Orphanage; below are the same brothers shortly before Trang's death. Source: Kianh Foundation Newsletter, Dec. 2011)

As a result of the use of Agent Orange, Vietnam estimates that over 400,000 people were killed or maimed, 500,000 children were born with birth defects, and up to 1 million people were disabled or suffered from health problems—not to mention the far-reaching impact it had on the health of over 3 million American troops and their offspring.

Internal Monsanto memos show that Monsanto knew of the problems of dioxin contamination of Agent Orange when it sold it to the U.S. government for use in Vietnam. Despite the widespread health impact, Monsanto and Dow were allowed to appeal for and receive financial protection from the U.S. government against veterans seeking compensation for their exposure to Agent Orange.

In 2012, a long 50 years after Agent Orange was deployed, the clean-up effort has finally begun. Yet the legacy of Agent Orange, and successive generations of body deformities, will remain in orphanages throughout VietNam for decades to come.

(Think that can't happen here? Two crops were recently genetically engineered to withstand a weedkiller made with one of the major components of Agent Orange, 2,4-D, in order to combat "super weeds" that evolved due to the excessive use of RoundUp.)

**8 –
Petroleum-Based Fertilizer**

In 1955, Monsanto began manufacturing petroleum-based fertilizer after purchasing a major oil refinery. Petroleum-based fertilizers can kill beneficial soil micro-organisms, sterilizing the soil and creating a dependence, like an addiction, to the synthetic replacements. Not the best addiction to have, considering the rising cost and dwindling supply of oil…

#9 – RoundUp

During the early 1970s, Monsanto founded their Agricultural Chemicals division with a focus on herbicides, and one herbicide in particular: RoundUp (glyphosate). Because of its ability to eradicate weeds literally overnight, RoundUp was quickly adopted by farmers. Its use increased even more when Monsanto introduced "RoundUp Ready" (glyphosate-resistant) crops, enabling farmers to saturate the entire field with weedkiller without killing the crops.

While glyphosate has been approved by regulatory bodies worldwide and is widely used, concerns about its effects on humans and the environment persist. RoundUp has been found in samples of groundwater, as well as soil, and even in streams and air throughout the Midwest U.S., and increasingly in food. It has been linked to butterfly mortality, and the proliferation of superweeds. Studies in rats have shown consistently negative health impacts ranging from tumors, altered organ function, and infertility, to cancer and premature death; click here to find countless study references to support these statements.

#10 –
Aspartame/NutraSweet/Equal

An accidental discovery during research on gastrointestinal hormones resulted in a uniquely sweet chemical: aspartame. During the clinical trials conducted on 7 infant monkeys as part of aspartame's application for FDA approval, 1 monkey died and 5 other monkeys had grand mal seizures—yet somehow aspartame was still approved by the FDA in 1974. In 1985, Monsanto acquired the company responsible for aspartame's manufacture (G.D. Searle) and began marketing the product as NutraSweet. Twenty years later, the U.S. Department of Health and Human Services released a report listing 94 health issues caused by aspartame. (Watch a quick video here.)

#11 —
Bovine Growth Hormone (rBGH)

This genetically modified hormone

was developed by Monsanto to be injected into dairy cows to produce more milk. Cows subjected to rBGH suffer excruciating pain due to swollen udders and mastitis, and the pus from the resulting infection enters the milk supply requiring the use of additional antibiotics. rBGH milk has been linked to breast cancer, colon cancer, and prostate cancer in humans.

#12 –
Genetically Modified Crops a.k.a. (GMOs)

In the early 1990s, Monsanto began gene-splicing corn, cotton, soy, and canola with DNA from viruses and bacteria in order to achieve one of two traits: an internally-generated pesticide (the corn or soy causes the insect's stomach to rupture if they eat it), or an internal resistance to

Monsanto's weedkiller RoundUp (enabling farmers to drench their field with RoundUp to kill ever-stronger weeds).

Despite decades of promises that genetically engineered crops would "feed the world" with "more nutrients," drought resistance, or yield, the majority of Monsanto's profits are from seeds that are engineered to tolerate Monsanto's RoundUp—providing them with an ever-increasing, dual income stream as weeds continue to evolve resistance to RoundUp.

Most sobering however, is that the world is once again buying into Monsanto's "safe" claims.

Just like the early days of PCBs, DDT, Agent Orange, Monsanto has successfully fooled the general public and regulatory agencies into believing that RoundUp, and the genetically modified crops that help sell RoundUp, are "safe." Despite the fact that NO human testing has ever been done on GMO crops!

Meanwhile, Monsanto has learned a thing or two in the past 100+ years of defending its dirty products: these days, when a new study shows the negative health or environmental impacts of GMOs, Monsanto attacks the study and its scientist(s) by flooding the media with counter claims from "independent" organizations, scientists, industry associations, blogs, sponsored social media, and articles by "private" public relations firms—all endorsed, founded, funded or maintained by Monsanto.

Unfortunately, few of us take the time to trace the members, founders, and relationships of these seemingly valid sources back to their little Monsanto secret. (Read more on this page.)

Fooling the FDA required a slightly different approach: click on the below chart compiled by Millions Against Monsanto to see how many former Monsanto VPs and legal counsel are now holding positions with the FDA. And don't forget Clarence Thomas, former Monsanto attorney who is now a Supreme Court Justice, ruling in favor of Monsanto in every case brought before him.

#13 –
Terminator Seeds

In the late 1990s, Monsanto developed the technology to produce sterile grains unable to germinate. The goal of these "Terminator Seeds" was to force farmers to buy new seeds from

Monsanto year after year, rather than save and reuse the seeds from their harvest as they've been doing throughout centuries.

Fortunately this technology never came to market. Instead, Monsanto managed to accomplish the same thing by requiring farmers to sign a binding contract agreeing that they will not save or sell seeds from year to year, which forces them to buy new seeds and preempts the need for a "terminator gene." Lucky for us... since the terminator seeds were capable of cross-pollination and could have contaminated local non-sterile crops.

Source References:

http://www.encyclopedia.com/topic/Monsanto_Company.aspx
http://www.chemheritage.org/discover/media/magazine/articles/28-1-the-pursuit-of-sweet.aspx?page=1
http://www.docstoc.com/docs/79474992/Re-Long-Term-Feeding-of-Sodium-Saccharin-to-Nonhuman-Primates
http://www.fas.org/ota/reports/7702.pdf
http://www.caloriecontrol.org/
http://www.cancer.gov/cancertopics/factsheet/Risk/artificial-sweeteners
http://www.cspinet.org/new/saccharin_delisted.html
http://ntp.niehs.nih.gov/ntp/roc/twelfth/appendices/AppendixB.pdf
http://www.chemheritage.org/discover/media/magazine/articles/28-1-the-pursuit-of-sweet.aspx
http://deepblue.lib.umich.edu/bitstream/handle/2027.42/33934/0000201.pdf;jsessionid=548799C31BFC89F058CEE9744E9790C4?sequence=1
http://www.greenfacts.org/en/pcbs/l-2/5-effects-animal.htm
http://www.epa.gov/osw/hazard/tsd/pcbs/pubs/effects.htm
http://www.foxriverwatch.com/monsanto2a_pcb_pcbs.html
http://worldwide.typepad.com/schoolhouse/2003/08/monsanto_optimi.html
http://www.ucsf.edu/news/2011/01/8371/ucsf-study-identifies-chemicals-pregnant-women
http://www.epa.gov/osw/hazard/wastetypes/pdfs/listing-ref.pdf
http://pubs.acs.org/doi/abs/10.1021/ac50124a019
https://en.wikipedia.org/wiki/Manhattan_Project
https://en.wikipedia.org/wiki/Dayton_Project
http://en.wikipedia.org/wiki/Texas_City_Disaster
http://www.who.int/mediacentre/factsheets/fs225/en/
http://www.hoianfoundation.org/images/NEWSLETTER%2011_06.pdf
http://www.thejournal.ie/agent-orange-clean-up-launched-in-vietnam-decades-after-war-ends-551652-Aug2012/
http://aaronjoelsantos.photoshelter.com/gallery/Agent-Orange-in-Vietnam/G0000t29aKsEmLSM
http://www.demotix.com/news/1299101/agent-orange-children-tudu-hospital-ho-chi-minh-city#media-1297827
http://www.organicconsumers.org/articles/article_26067.cfm
http://pmep.cce.cornell.edu/profiles/extoxnet/24d-captan/24d-ext.html
http://environment.nationalgeographic.com/environment/green-

guide/buying-guides/fertilizer/environmental-impact/
http://www.ncbi.nlm.nih.gov/pubmed/22101424
http://www.non-gmoreport.com/articles/jan10/scientists_find_negative_impacts_of_GM_crops.php
http://www.reuters.com/article/2011/08/31/us-glyphosate-pollution-idUSTRE77U61720110831
http://www.pages.drexel.edu/%7Els39/peer_review/losey1.htm
http://www.theatlantic.com/health/archive/2012/05/superweeds-a-long-predicted-problem-for-gm-crops-has-arrived/257187/
http://gmo-awareness.com/all-about-gmos/gmo-risks/
http://us.rd.yahoo.com/dailynews/ygreen/sc_ygreen/storytext/eightwaysmonsantoisdestroyingourhealth/40903884/SIG=114jsp1h4/*http://www.dorway.com/badnews.html#symptoms
http://www.psr.org/chapters/oregon/assets/pdfs/rbghs-harmful-effects-on.pdf
http://www.motherearthnews.com/happy-homesteader/GMOs-rBGH-milk-zboz10zkon.aspx#axzz2PjlPXLfa
http://gmo-awareness.com/all-about-gmos/gmo-defined/
http://grist.org/article/food-2010-10-06-court-rules-on-rbgh-free-milk/
http://www.cof.orst.edu/cof/teach/agbio2009/Readings%202009/Parodi%20Dairy%20Cancer%20rGBH%20J%20Am%20Coll%20Nutrition%202005.pdf
http://www.preventcancer.com/consumers/general/milk.htm
http://www.yourhealthbase.com/milk_cancer.htm
http://www.bloomberg.com/news/2013-04-03/monsanto-raises-forecast-as-profit-tops-estimates-on-corn-seed.html
http://www.reuters.com/article/2012/05/10/us-agriculture-weeds-idUSBRE8491JZ20120510
http://gmo-awareness.com/all-about-gmos/gmo-fda/
http://www.organicconsumers.org/monsanto/
http://en.wikipedia.org/wiki/Genetic_use_restriction_technology
http://www.prnewswire.com/news-releases/studies-show-gmos-in-majority-of-us-processed-foods-58-percent-of-americans-unaware-of-issue-104510549.html
http://articles.chicagotribune.com/2012-08-04/news/ct-met-gmo-sweet-corn-20120804_1_sweet-corn-food-allergies-patty-lovera
http://us.rd.yahoo.com/dailynews/ygreen/sc_ygreen/storytext/eightwaysmonsantoisdestroyingourhealth/40903884/SIG=11hilmku0/*http://www.organicconsumers.org/bytes/ob258.htm
http://www.organicconsumers.org/articles/article_23470.cfm
https://www.facebook.com/gmoawarenessusa

http://drleonardcoldwell.com/2014/01/20/monsantos-dirty-dozen/?print=print

SOURCE:

http://truththeory.com/2014/01/20/monsantos-dirty-dozen/

The Monsanto Legacy?

Between 75% to 80% of the processed food you consume every day has GMOs inside, and residues of Monsanto's RoundUp herbicide outside. But it's not just processed food—fresh fruit and vegetables are next: genetically engineered sweet corn is already being sold at your local grocer, with apples and a host of other "natural" produce currently in field trials.

How is it that Monsanto is allowed to manipulate our food after such a dark product history? How is it they are allowed to cause such detrimental impact to our environment and our health?

According to the Organic Consumers Association, "There is a direct correlation between our genetically engineered food supply and the $2 trillion the U.S. spends annually on medical care, namely an epidemic of diet-related chronic diseases.

Instead of healthy fruits, vegetables, grains, and grass-fed animal products, U.S. factory farms and food processors produce a glut of genetically engineered junk foods that generate heart disease, stroke, diabetes and cancer—backed by farm subsidies—while organic farmers receive no such subsidies.

Monsanto's history reflects a consistent pattern of toxic chemicals, lawsuits, and manipulated science. Is this the kind of company we want controlling our world's food supply?

P.S. Monsanto's not alone. Other companies in the "Big Six" include Pioneer Hi-Bred

International (a subsidiary of DuPont), Syngenta AG, Dow Agrosciences (a subsidiary of Dow Chemical, BASF (which is primarily a chemical company that is rapidly expanding their biotechnology division), and Bayer Cropscience (a subsidiary of Bayer). The website Biofortified.org maintains a complete list of companies doing genetic engineering.

Chapter 5
A Dark eMail

Denise began...

1st about the Monsanto Protection Act: H.R. 933 which was passed into law March 21, 2013 that ensures Monsanto cannot be prosecuted for crimes against humanity – which screams volumes about the politicians we vote into office.

Look it up!

Now...

The Dark Act

The title is not a joke! I know you are tired of listening to my seeming rantings and ravings and conspiricy theories – but – just promise me that you'll read this and consider the source.

Please – just read it!!

All my love, Denise!

◊◊◊

5 Things To Know . . .

The Safe and Accurate Food Labeling Act of 2015 moving through the House of Representatives would have major implications on GMO labeling and crop production.
By <u>Anna Roth</u> on <u>July 20, 2015</u>
Filed Under: <u>GMOs</u>

The Safe and Accurate Food Labeling Act of 2015 moving through the House of Representatives would have major implications on GMO labeling and crop production.

Update*: After we published this article, several House Democrats [filed amendments](#), potentially disabling several key parts of the bill. What you see below refers to the bill's original language.*

There are two names for [H.R. 1599](#), the controversial Republican-backed bill concerning [GMO](#) labeling that is currently moving through the House of Representatives.

The first is its bland, official name: The Safe and Accurate Food Labeling Act of 2015. The second is the nickname given by its opponents: Deny Americans the Right to Know (DARK) Act. Together, they reveal the two sides in the frequently bitter fight about the safety of genetically modified food.

Critics of GMOs have a long list of concerns. Take Monsanto's notorious "Roundup Ready" seeds. They have been bred to resist an herbicide recently deemed a "probable carcinogen" by the World Health Organization; they have led to a rise in monoculture crop production; and they have been linked to the decline of the Monarch butterfly. Critics also worry about genetic contamination and a lack of research into the long-term health effects of the crops.

For these reasons and more, two economists recently called GMOs "perhaps the greatest case of human hubris ever" in a New York Times editorial, saying agriculture industry has created a system "too big to fail," much like the banking industry in 2008.

Meanwhile, GMO supporters argue that the world is facing a global hunger crisis, and foods genetically modified to have more nutrients could be potential lifesavers.

But H.R. 1599 is not about the existence of GMOs, which are entrenched in American agriculture (GMO crops account for around 90 percent of corn and soy grown in the country). It's about whether the genetically modified foods you buy should be labeled as such. And because independent poll after poll shows that the majority of Americans support GMO labeling, the bill's opponents see the bill as nothing more than the agrochemical industry flexing its lobbying muscles.

The bill passed through the House Agriculture Committee last week, and will go up for debate on the House floor as early as next week; many in the industry expect the House to get to it before the August recess. Here's what you need to know about the so-called DARK Act and how it affects GMO labeling and production as a whole:

1. It would negate all existing GMO labeling laws.

Most of the legislature around GMO labeling has been designed to alert consumers to the presence of genetically modified ingredients, which the Center for Food Safety estimates are in at least 70 percent of processed food. Pesticide and seed companies like Monsanto and industry groups like the Grocery Manufacturers Association have spent millions defeating pro-labeling bills in several states, including

California, Washington, Colorado and Oregon.

Despite the industry's deep pockets, a law passed in Vermont last year that would require mandatory GMO labeling for all ingredients by July 2016. Connecticut and Maine have also both passed bills requiring labeling, but they can only take effect once enough states nearby have similar laws. H.R. 1599 would negate all of these laws, and more—according to the Center for Food Safety. The preemption language in the bill would nullify over a hundred local laws that, directly or indirectly, regulate genetically engineered crops.

There's nothing stopping food companies from doing their own labeling. But as Ken Roseboro, editor and publisher of the *The Organic & Non-GMO Report* points out, they've had this power since 2001, when the FDA issued guidance on voluntary GMO and non-GMO labeling. "How many companies have voluntarily labeled their products as containing GMOs since then? None," he says.

2. The bill would give jurisdiction over non-GMO certification to the U.S. Department of Agriculture (USDA), which doesn't have the same rigor as independent certification programs.

Because of public perception around GMOs, companies are much more likely to advertise the *absence* of genetically modified ingredients in their products—whether they're big corporations like Chipotle and General Mills, or small food companies using labels like the butterfly and checkmark logo of the Non-GMO Project, an independent nonprofit.

H.R. 1599 would put the system of voluntary non-GMO certification under the jurisdiction of the USDA. The USDA already has its own (new) certification program, which is much less rigorous than the Non-GMO Projects and doesn't require testing or segregation. If the bill passes, however, independent verifiers would essentially use the USDA's standards and process (much like with the federal organic standards). No one knows whether the new USDA verification process will take longer, cost more, or be more onerous than independent verifications. (A previous version of the bill had language that would block private GMO-free labels, but that has been taken out of the current draft.)

3. There is language in the bill that preempts state and local laws regarding the *production* of GMO crops, not just labeling.

To opponents of the bill, this is far more sinister than the labeling laws. As a response to concerns about the health and environmental effects of GMOs, a few counties in California and Oregon have led grassroots efforts and passed laws that limit genetically engineered crop production or even [establish "GMO-free zones."](#)

H.R. 1599 would overturn all of these laws and preempt new ones from taking their place. "It removes local control over GMOs from citizens," says Roseboro.

4. The bill would expand the definition of "natural" to

include some genetically modified ingredients.

The natural label is something of a joke in the industry, because it means so little; many highly processed foods can be considered "natural," and unlike organic, there isn't an official verification process behind the term. But there is language in H.R. 1599 that allows companies to make "natural" claims on packaging even if the food contains GMOs.

Opponents of the bill believe that it will add to consumer confusion. A Consumer Reports survey found that nearly 60 percent of shoppers look for the "natural" label on foods and more than 75 percent of them believe that the label has specific attributes like lack of artificial coloring, flavor, or GMOs–even though it has no legal definition.

5. Even if the bill is introduced in the Senate, it probably won't pass—and there are bills in both the House and Senate in favor of mandatory labeling.

As we all know, a bill needs to pass in both the House and Senate before it becomes a law. The Senate corollary to H.R. 1599 hasn't been introduced at press time, though many expect it to appear any day now. But experts say the odds of it finding enough Democratic backing in the Senate are slim—and it would still need to be signed into law by President Obama.

In February, Democrats in both the House and Senate introduced bills that would require mandatory national GMO labeling administered by the U.S. Food and Drug Administration (FDA).

Neither is as far along as H.R. 1599, but they represent hope for those who believe in GMO labeling on the federal level. See the latest on state-level labeling efforts here.

Source Reference:

http://civileats.com/2015/07/20/5-things-to-know-about-the-dark-act/

Addendum

The Ultimate Killing Machine – GMOs

By Stephanie Relfe

Activist Post

It looks the same — the bread, pies, sodas, even corn on the cob. So much of what we eat every day looks just like it did 20 years ago. But something profoundly different has happened without our knowledge or consent. And according to leading doctors, what we don't know is already hurting us big time.

What are GMOs? -- GMO stands for "Genetically Modified Organism". Sometimes the initials "GM" are used, which stands for

"Genetically Modified". Genetic engineering is very different from normal breeding because it involves taking genes from a completely different species and inserting them into the DNA of another species of plant or even of an animal.

Organic Dairy Farmer, Paul Fonder, decided to do a second feeding study with GMO corn v Organic corn in his barn in South Dakota. The mice got to work while Paul was busy on the farm this spring. Three months later, not even a nibble taken out of the GMO corn.

We smell a rat. And maybe the rat smells formaldehyde?

Corn set out, early April

Three months later...

For the first time in history, bacteria, plants and animals can all be mixed up together. For example, right now the DNA of bacteria is put into food plants. The two primary reasons plants are genetically engineered are to allow them to:

1. *Drink* poison, or
2. *Produce* poison

The poison drinkers are inserted with genes from bacteria that allow them to survive otherwise deadly doses of herbicides. The main poison in GMOs is glyphosate, the poison that is in Roundup. Biotech companies sell the seed and herbicide as a package deal, and farmers can then use hundreds of millions of pounds more herbicide than would normally be possible without the plants dying.

The poison producers are called Bt crops. Inserted genes from the a bacteria produce a pesticide (poison) in every cell of the plant.

What kills insects, kills us. This is a pesticide which is INSIDE the plant. **You cannot wash it off!**

More than 70% of the foods on supermarket shelves contain GM foods. Get a magnifying glass and read the list of ingredients. Unless the following words are organic, do not eat it.

- Corn
- Soy
- Canola (Rapeseed. This is toxic and should not be eaten in any case)
- Cotton seed (This is toxic and should not be eaten in any case)
- Sugar (beet sugar is GMO. Cane sugar so far is okay)
- Hawaiian papaya
- Zucchini & crook neck squash

Other countries have or import GMO rice and potato. But it gets worse. Since we now have genetically modified alfalfa, and alfalfa, corn and soy are fed to animals, unless it's organic, you must not eat:

- Dairy
- Meat
- Eggs
- Farm-raised fish or seafood

Glyphosate has even been found in the bodies of [dairy cows in Denmark](), because Europe imports GMO feed! So you know it has to be in the milk.

This is why we no longer eat out anywhere. Since no restaurant uses organic, GMO-free food, or gives you a full list of ingredients, you are bound to be eating poison in virtually every restaurant, fast-food joint and school canteen.

Organic food is meant to be free of GMOs. But we are starting to find out that even this is not a guarantee. It's way too easy to sneak in. There have been so far at least two instances discovered where GMOs were found in so-called 'organic' food. In each case, this discovery was not made by organizations that should protect you, like the FDA. They were made by independent bodies. [Baby food is one](). Which is really scary. The only food a baby should have is breast milk and, when ready for solids, homemade baby food (cook it, strain it, freeze in ice cube trays) and reverse osmosis water.

Kashi 'organic' cereal is another. The Cornucopia Institute found that **Kashi has high levels of GMOs in its '[organic]() cereal**. You may be less surprised at this once you realize that Kashi is not owned by nature-lovers, but by Kellogg's.

∞

Animals Fed GMO Corn for Two Years

GROW MASSIVE TUMORS

In the first long-term study of GMOs, rats fed a lifelong diet of one of genetically modified corn grew tumors and had multiple organ damage, of the liver and kidneys.

Corn is meant to be nutritious. It is not meant to do this –

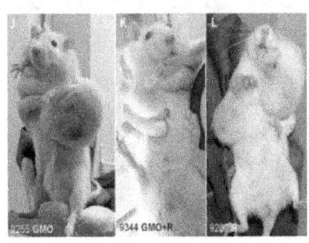

ANIMALS FED GMOs

Have

Sterile Grandchildren

When Genetically Modified Organisms (GMOs) were first created, some people knew they were very bad. But no one really knew just how bad they are. We know that now. Basically, not only are they killing people, because they are so highly toxic, they are also doing something VERY DIFFERENT TO NORMAL FOOD, that in the longer term they will wipe out the human race if not eradicated completely. **Because animals fed GMOs do not have great grandchildren.** NO other toxic food does that! This is proof that we are dealing with something completely different. *And evil.* Here is some evidence of this:

Concerning the experiment carried out jointly by the National Association for Gene Security and the Institute of Ecological and Evolutional Problems, Dr. Alexei Surov had this to say.

"We selected several groups of hamsters, kept them in pairs in cells and gave them ordinary food as always," says Alexei Surov.

"We did not add anything for one group but the other was fed with soya that contained no GM components, while the third group with some content of Genetically Modified Organisms and the fourth one with increased amount of GMO. We monitored their behavior and how they gain weight and when they give birth to their cubs. Originally, everything went smoothly. However, we noticed quite a serious effect when we selected new pairs from their cubs and continued to feed them as before. These pairs' growth rate was slower and they reached their sexual maturity more slowly. When we got some of their cubs we formed the new pairs of the third generation. We failed to get cubs from these pairs, which were fed with GM foodstuffs. It was proved that these pairs lost their ability to give birth to their cubs," Dr. Alexei Surov said.

Another surprise was discovered by scientists in hamsters of the third generation. Hair grew in the mouth of the animals that took part in the experiment.

GMOs remain inside of us

The only published human feeding study revealed one of the most dangerous problems from GM foods. The gene inserted into GM soy transfers into the DNA of bacteria living inside our intestines . . . and continues to function. This means that long after we stop eating GMOs, we may still have potentially harmful GM proteins produced continuously inside of us.

Put more plainly, eating a corn chip produced from Bt corn might transform our intestinal bacteria into living pesticide factories, possibly for the rest of our lives.

Please, get this information to all your family and friends!

GMOs Destroy Organs

If GMOs did nothing, then organs of animals fed GMOs should look exactly the same as normal. But they look radically different, as you can see from [this photo]():

If that still does not convince you that it is deadly serious that you become obsessive about getting

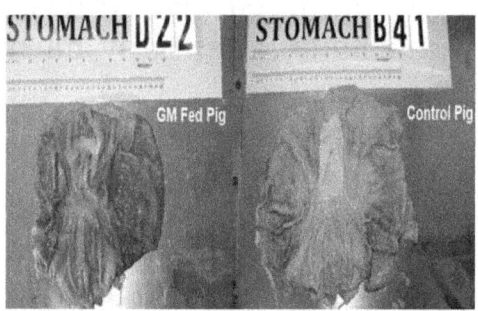

GMOs out of your diet, here's another pic that proves that GMOs seriously alter the whole body. This photo is a comparison of rat testicles:

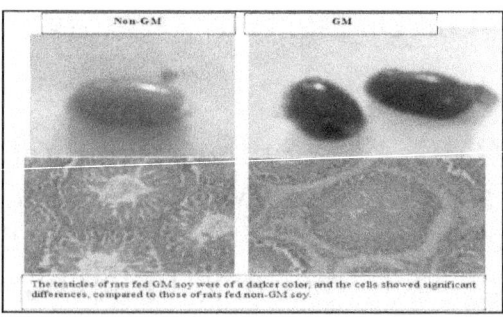

People are dying at very early ages, and you know from seeing these pictures of totally changed organs, that GMOs are a major, if not THE major cause, behind it. You won't hear about this in the media, because the power of Monsanto goes nearly everywhere. The following are just a few examples that I have collected:

My 40 year old female cousin died of breast cancer tonight . . .

Her parents raised her on a healthy diet, totally healthy. They took supplements, had a garden, went to church, didn't drink or smoke EVER...and then one day she finds a lump.

She decided to treat it using natural methods like Vitamin C treatments, oxygenation, hydrogen peroxide, changing the body to alkaline, all under the supervision of natural healers and doctors...but she was also getting chemo treatments.

She ate an organic diet and cleansed weekly to flush the poison from her body and kept her immune system boosted to fight off infection. She was totally informed about modern day, alternative, cancer treatments, and what she was doing to beat it.

A week and a half ago she was admitted into the hospital with severe pain from fluid gathering around her heart and lungs (the tumor area). Doctors drained her chest and tested the fluid and found it to be full of cancer cells, all of the sudden it spread, it had taken over.

A week and a half ago she was a beautiful, youthful 40 year old woman and today she is dead.

She looked 80 years old when I saw her earlier today at the hospital. From 40 to 80 in a week and a half.... What the ---- is going on around here people?!

(Note: All you have to do is look again at the pictures of the tumors on the rats, and change to the organs from GMOs, and you will know).

On another post, I read about a lady who walked into her boyfriend's house, and found him dead in the middle of the living room. He was only 40 years old.

A lady I talked with in the line at the post office said that 5 people, all close to her and most of them under 50, had all died in the last month.

Another poster said that 6 people close to them, none of them particularly old, had all died within several months of each other.

Something is causing this. Vaccines are part of the cause, but GMOs are obviously deadly. The mainstream media will not tell you that GMOs are killing people. I urge you to totally get GMOs and all other toxins out of your life.

GMOs is just one of the 55 chapters in the book that I spent 2 years writing - You're not Fat, You're Toxic - to help you save you and your family. If you don't want to buy it, I suggest that you ask the library to obtain a copy:

You're Not Fat - You're Toxic

Amazon Review by Borce, a Homeopath in Macedonia,

who has 500 Holistic Books: "The Best Book I have ever Read... The Book of the Century"

More information on GMOs:

- GMOs in Beer
- GMOs by Country
- GMO genes are jumping species!
- Boycott these Companies that are Pro-GMO
- Scientists get Fired for Finding that GMOs are Really Bad for us
- Kevlar Tires now required to Traverse "Spear-like" GMO crops
- GMO Bananas, Rice, Potatoes, Sugar Cane are on the wayThe Non-GMO Project
-

Stephanie Relfe was born in Sydney, Australia in 1960. She has a Bachelor of Science degree from Sydney University where she majored in Histology (the study of cells) and Zoology. Stephanie has had over 200 hours in training in Specialized Kinesiology and over 100 hours training in Clearing, a technology which helps a person to improve their thoughts and actions using a biofeedback meter. She has worked as a professional Specialized Kinesiologist since 1993, both in Australia and the USA. Stephanie has developed her own method of Specialized Kinesiology called Synergistic Kinesiology. She is married to Michael Relfe from the USA and has a son. Her websites include:

- www.Relfe.com
- www.SynergisticKinesiology.com
- www.PerfectHealthSystem.com
- www.PerfectHealthDVD.com
- www.YoureNotFatYoureToxic.com

The World's "Most Evil Corporation"

By E Hanzai
Global Research, May 20, 2015
Waking Times 22 June 2014

Of all the mega-corps running amok, Monsanto has consistently outperformed its rivals, earning the crown as "most evil corporation on Earth!" Not content to simply rest upon its throne of destruction, it remains focused on newer, more scientifically innovative ways to harm the planet and its people.

1901: The company is founded by John Francis Queeny, a member of the Knights of Malta, a thirty year pharmaceutical veteran married to Olga Mendez Monsanto, for which Monsanto Chemical Works is named. The company's first product is chemical saccharin, sold to Coca-Cola as an artificial sweetener.

Even then, the government knew saccharin was poisonous and sued to stop its manufacture but lost in court, thus opening the Monsanto Pandora's Box to begin poisoning the world through the soft drink.

Wife of Founder of Monsanto Company John Francis Queeny: "Olga Mendez Monsanto" Mother of Edgar Monsanto & Olguita Monsanto. Olga is allegedly the daughter of Don Emmanuel Mendes de Monsanto of Spanish Sephardic Jewish descent who financed her husband's John's Monsanto Chemical Company. Her alleged mother was a German named Emma Cleaves. She allegedly was born in 1870 on St. Thomas and died in England in 1938.

Founder of Monsanto Company, alleged Irish-American Roman Catholic John Francis Queeny August 17, 1859 – March 19, 1933 According to the Count in Venice, John Francis Queeny was a Knight of Malta.

1920s: Monsanto expands into industrial chemicals and drugs, becoming the world's largest maker of aspirin, acetylsalicyclic acid, (toxic of course). This is also the time when things began to go horribly wrong for the planet in a hurry with the introduction of their polychlorinated biphenyls (PCBs).

> "PCBs were considered an industrial wonder chemical, an oil that wouldn't burn, impervious to degradation and had almost limitless applications. Today PCBs are considered one of the gravest chemical threats on the planet. Widely used as lubricants, hydraulic fluids, cutting oils, waterproof coatings and liquid sealants,

are potent carcinogens and have been implicated in reproductive, developmental and immune system disorders. The world's center of PCB manufacturing was Monsanto's plant on the outskirts of East St. Louis, Illinois, which has the highest rate of fetal death and immature births in the state."

Even though PCBs were eventually banned after fifty years for causing such devastation, it is still present in just about all animal and human blood and tissue cells across the globe. Documents introduced in court later showed Monsanto was fully aware of the deadly effects, but criminally hid them from the public to keep the PCB gravy-train going full speed!

1930s: Created its first hybrid seed corn and expands into detergents, soaps, industrial cleaning products, synthetic rubbers and plastics. Oh yes, all toxic of course!

1940s: They begin research on uranium to be used for the Manhattan Project's first atomic bomb, which would later be dropped on Hiroshima and Nagasaki, killing hundreds of thousands of Japanese, Korean and US Military servicemen and poisoning millions more.

The company continues its unabated killing spree by creating pesticides for agriculture containing deadly dioxin, which poisons the food and water supplies. It was later discovered Monsanto failed to disclose that dioxin was used in a wide range of their products because doing so would force them to acknowledge that it had created an environmental Hell on Earth.

1950s: Closely aligned with The Walt Disney Company, Monsanto creates several attractions at Disney's Tomorrowland, espousing the glories of chemicals and plastics. Their "House of the Future" is constructed entirely of toxic plastic that is not biodegradable as they had asserted. What, Monsanto lied? I'm shocked!

> "After attracting a total of 20 million visitors from 1957 to 1967, Disney finally tore the house down, but discovered it would not go down without a fight. According to

Monsanto Magazine, wrecking balls literally bounced off the glass-fiber, reinforced polyester material. Torches, jackhammers, chain saws and shovels did not work. Finally, choker cables were used to squeeze off parts of the house bit by bit to be trucked away."

Monsanto's Disneyfied vision of the future:

1960s: Monsanto, along with chemical partner-in-crime DOW Chemical, produces dioxin-laced Agent Orange for use in the U.S.'s Vietnam invasion. The results? Over 3 million people contaminated, a half-million Vietnamese civilians dead, a half-million Vietnamese babies born with birth defects and thousands of U.S. military veterans suffering or dying from its effects to this day!

Monsanto is hauled into court again and internal memos show they knew the deadly effects of dioxin in Agent Orange when they sold it to the government. Outrageously though, Monsanto is allowed to present their own "research" that concluded dioxin was safe and posed no negative health concerns whatsoever. Satisfied, the bought and paid for courts side with Monsanto and throws the case out. Afterwards, it comes to light that Monsanto lied about the findings and their real research concluded that dioxin kills very effectively.

A later internal memo released in a 2002 trial admitted

"that the evidence proving the persistence of these compounds and their universal presence as residues in the environment is beyond question ... the public and legal pressures to eliminate them to prevent global contamination are inevitable. The subject is snowballing. Where do we go from here? The alternatives: go out of business; sell the hell out of them as long as we can and do nothing else; try to stay in business; have alternative products."

Monsanto partners with I.G. Farben, makers of Bayer aspirin and the Third Reich's go-to chemical manufacturer producing deadly Zyklon-B gas during World War II. Together, the companies use their collective expertise to introduce aspartame, another extremely deadly neurotoxin, into the food supply. When questions surface regarding the toxicity of saccharin, Monsanto exploits this opportunity to introduce yet another of its deadly poisons onto an unsuspecting public.

1970s: Monsanto partner, G.D. Searle, produces numerous internal studies which claim aspartame to be safe, while the FDA's own scientific research clearly reveals that aspartame causes tumors and massive holes in the brains of rats, before killing them. The FDA initiates a grand jury investigation into G.D. Searle for "knowingly misrepresenting findings and concealing material facts and making false statements" in regard to aspartame safety.

During this time, Searle strategically taps prominent Washington insider Donald Rumsfeld, who served as Secretary of Defense during the Gerald Ford and George W. Bush presidencies, to become CEO. The corporation's primary goal is to have Rumsfeld utilize his political influence and vast experience in the killing business to grease the FDA to play ball with them.

A few months later, Samuel Skinner receives "an offer he can't refuse," withdraws from the investigation and resigns his post at the U.S. Attorney's Office to go work for Searle's law firm. This mob tactic stalls the case just long enough for the statute of limitation to run out and the grand jury investigation is abruptly and conveniently dropped.

1980s: Amid indisputable research that reveals the toxic effects of aspartame and as then FDA commissioner Dr. Jere Goyan was about to sign a petition into law keeping it off the market, Donald Rumsfeld calls Ronald Reagan for a favor the day after he takes office. Reagan fires the uncooperative Goyan and appoints Dr. Arthur Hayes Hull to head the FDA, who then quickly tips the scales in Searle's favor and NutraSweet is approved for human consumption in dried products. This becomes sadly ironic since Reagan, a known jelly bean and candy enthusiast, later suffers from Alzheimers during his second term, one of the many horrific effects of aspartame consumption.

Searle's real goal though was to have aspartame approved as a soft drink sweetener since exhaustive studies revealed that at temperatures exceeding 85 degrees Fahrenheit, it "breaks down into known toxins Diketopiperazines (DKP), methyl (wood) alcohol, and formaldehyde."(4), becoming many times deadlier than its powdered form!

The National Soft Drink Association (NSDA) is initially in an uproar, fearing future lawsuits from consumers permanently injured or killed by drinking the poison. When Searle is able to show that liquid aspartame, though incredibly deadly, is much more addictive than crack cocaine, the NSDA is convinced that skyrocketing profits from the sale of soft drinks laced with aspartame would easily offset any future liability. With that, corporate greed wins and the unsuspecting soft drink consumers pay for it with damaged healths.

Coke leads the way once again (remember saccharin?) and begins poisoning Diet Coke drinkers with aspartame in 1983. As expected, sales skyrocket as millions become hopelessly addicted and sickened by the sweet poison served in a can. The rest of the soft drink industry likes what it sees and quickly follows suit, conveniently forgetting all about their initial reservations that aspartame is a deadly chemical. There's money to be made, lots of it and that's all that really matters to them anyway!

In 1985, undaunted by the swirl of corruption and multiple accusations of fraudulent research undertaken by Searle, Monsanto purchases the company and forms a new aspartame subsidiary called NutraSweet Company. When multitudes of independent scientists and researchers continue to warn about aspartame's toxic effects, Monsanto goes on the offensive, bribing the National Cancer Institute and providing their own fraudulent papers to get the NCI to claim that formaldehyde does not cause cancer so that aspartame can stay on the market.

The known effects of aspartame ingestion are: "mania, rage, violence, blindness, joint-pain, fatigue, weight-gain, chest-pain, coma, insomnia, numbness, depression, tinnitus, weakness, spasms, irritability, nausea, deafness, memory-loss, rashes, dizziness, headaches, seizures, anxiety, palpitations, fainting, cramps, diarrhoea, panic, burning in the mouth. Diseases triggered/mimmicked include diabetes, MS, lupus, epilepsy, Parkinson's, tumours, miscarriage, infertility, fibromyalgia, infant death, Alzheimer's... Source : U.S. Food & Drug Administration.(5)

Further, 80% of complaints made to the FDA regarding food additives are about aspartame, which is now in over 5,000 products including diet and non-diet sodas and sports drinks, mints, chewing gum, frozen desserts, cookies, cakes, vitamins, pharmaceuticals, milk drinks, instant teas, coffees, yogurt, baby food and many, many more!(6) Read labels closely and do not buy anything that contains this horrific killer!

Amidst all the death and disease, FDA's Arthur Hull resigns under a cloud of corruption and is immediately hired by Searle's public relations firm as a senior scientific consultant. No, that's not a joke! Monsanto, the FDA and many government health regulatory agencies have become one and the same! It seems the only prerequisite for becoming an FDA commissioner is that they spend time at either Monsanto or one of the pharmaceutical cartel's organized crime corps.

1990s: Monsanto spends millions defeating state and federal legislation that disallows the corporation from continuing to dump dioxins, pesticides and other cancer-causing poisons into drinking water systems. Regardless, they are sued countless times for causing disease in their plant workers, the people in surrounding areas and birth defects in babies.

With their coffins full from the massive billions of profits, the $100 million dollar settlements are considered the low cost of doing business and thanks to the FDA, Congress and White House, business remains very good. So good that Monsanto is sued for giving radioactive iron to 829 pregnant women for a study to see what would happen to them.

In 1994, the FDA once again criminally approves Monsanto's latest monstrosity, the Synthetic Bovine Growth Hormone (rBGH), produced from a genetically modified E. coli bacteria, despite obvious outrage from the scientific community of its dangers. Of course, Monsanto claims that diseased pus milk, full of antibiotics and hormones is not only safe, but actually good for you!

Worse yet, dairy companies who refuse to use this toxic cow pus and label their products as "rBGH-free" are sued by Monsanto, claiming it gives them an unfair advantage over competitors that did. In essence, what Monsanto was saying is "yeah, we know rBGH makes people sick, but it's not alright that you advertise it's not in your products."

The following year, the diabolical company begins producing GMO crops that are tolerant to their toxic herbicide Roundup. Roundup-ready canola oil (rapeseed), soybeans, corn and BT cotton begin hitting the market, advertised as being safer, healthier alternatives to their organic non-GMO rivals. Apparently, the propaganda worked as today over 80% of canola on the market is their GMO variety.

A few things you definitely want to avoid in your diet are GMO soy, corn, wheat and canola oil, despite the fact that many "natural" health experts claim the latter to be a healthy oil. It's not, but you'll find it polluting many products on grocery store shelves.

Because these GM crops have been engineered to 'self-pollinate,' they do not need nature or bees to do that for them. There is a very dark side agenda to this and that is to wipe out the world's bee population.

Monsanto knows that birds and especially bees, throw a wrench into their monopoly due to their ability to pollinate plants, thus naturally creating foods outside of the company's "full domination control agenda." When bees attempt to pollinate a GM plant or flower, it gets poisoned and dies.

In fact, the bee colony collapse was recognized and has been going on since GM crops were first introduced.

To counter the accusations that they deliberately caused this ongoing genocide of bees, Monsanto devilishly buys out Beeologics, the largest bee research firm that was dedicated to studying the colony collapse phenomenon and whose extensive research named the monster as the primary culprit! After that, it's "bees, what bees? Everything's just dandy!" Again, I did not make this up, but wish I had!

During the mid-90s, they decide to reinvent their evil company as one focused on controlling the world's food supply through artificial, biotechnology means to preserve the Roundup cash-cow from losing market-share in the face of competing, less-toxic herbicides. You see, Roundup is so toxic that it wipes out non-GMO crops, insects, animals, human health and the environment at the same time. How very efficient!

Because Roundup-ready crops are engineered to be toxic pesticides masquerading as food, they have been banned in the EU, but not in America! Is there any connection between that and the fact that Americans, despite the high cost and availability of healthcare, are collectively the sickest people in the world? Of course not!

As was Monsanto's plan from the beginning, all non-Monsanto crops would be destroyed, forcing farmers the world over to use only its toxic [terminator seeds](). And Monsanto made sure farmers who refused to come into the fold were driven out of business or sued when windblown terminator seeds poisoned organic farms.

This gave the company a virtual monopoly as terminator seed crops and Roundup worked hand in glove with each other as GMO crops could not survive in a non-chemical environment so farmers were forced to buy both.

Their next step was to spend billions globally buying up as many seed companies as possible and transitioning them into terminator seed companies in an effort to wipe out any rivals and eliminate organic foods off the face of the earth. In Monsanto's view, all foods must be under their full control and genetically modified or they are not safe to eat!

They pretend to be shocked that their critics in the scientific community question whether crops genetically modified with the genes of diseased pigs, cows, spiders, monkeys, fish, vaccines and viruses are healthy to eat. The answer to that question is obviously a very big "no way!"

You'd think the company would be so proud of their GMO foods that they'd serve them to their employees, but they don't. In fact, [Monsanto has banned GM foods](#) from being served in their own employee cafeterias. Monsanto lamely responded "we believe in choice." What they really means is "we don't want to kill the help."

It's quite okay though to force-feed poor nations and Americans these modified monstrosities as a means to end starvation since dead people don't need to eat! I'll bet the thought on most peoples' minds these days is that Monsanto is clearly focused on eugenics and genocide, as opposed to providing foods that will sustain the world. As in Monsanto partner Disney's Sleeping Beauty, the wicked witch gives the people the poisoned GMO apple that puts them to sleep forever!

2000s: By this time Monsanto controls the largest share of the global GMO market. In turn, the US gov't spends hundreds of millions to fund aerial spraying of Roundup, causing massive environmental devastation. Fish and animals by the thousands die within days of spraying as respiratory ailments and cancer deaths in humans spike tremendously. But this is all considered an unusual coincidence so the spraying continues. If you thought Monsanto and the FDA were one and the same, well you can add the gov't to that sorry list now.

The monster grows bigger: Monsanto merges with Pharmacia & Upjohn, then separates from its chemical business and rebrands itself as an agricultural company. Yes, that's right, a chemical company whose products have devastated the environment, killed millions of people and wildlife over the years now wants us to believe they produce safe and nutritious foods that won't kill people any longer. That's an extremely hard-sell, which is why they continue to grow bigger through mergers and secret partnerships.

Because rival DuPont is too large a corporation to be allowed to merge with, they instead form a stealth partnership where each agrees to drop existing patent lawsuits against one another and begin sharing GMO technologies for mutual benefit. In layman's terms, together they would be far too powerful and politically connected for anything to stop them from owning a virtual monopoly on agriculture; "control the food supply & you control the people!"

Not all is rosy as the monster is repeatedly sued for $100s of millions for causing illness, infant deformities and death by illegally dumping all manner of PCBs into ground water, and continually lying about products safety – you know, business as usual.

The monster often perseveres and proves difficult to slay as it begins filing <u>frivolous suits against farmers</u> it claims infringe on their terminator seed patents. In virtually all cases, unwanted <u>seeds are windblown onto farmers'</u>

lands by neighboring terminator-seeded farms. Not only do these horrendous seeds destroy the organic farmers' crops, the lawsuits drive them into bankruptcy, while the Supreme Court overturns lower court rulings and sides with Monsanto each time.

At the same time, the monster begins filing patents on breeding techniques for pigs, claiming animals bred any way remotely similar to their patent would grant them ownership. So loose was this patent filing that it became obvious they wanted to claim all pigs bred throughout the world would infringe upon their patent.

The global terrorism spreads to India as over 100,000 farmers who are bankrupted by GMO crop failure, commit suicide by drinking Roundup so their families will be eligible for death insurance payments. In response, the monster takes advantage of the situation by alerting the media to a new project to assist small Indian farmers by donating the very things that caused crop failures in the country in the first place! Forbes then names Monsanto "company of the year." Sickening, but true.

More troubling is that Whole Foods, the corporation that brands itself as organic, natural and eco-friendly is proven to be anything but. They refuse to support Proposition 37, California's GMO-labeling measure that Monsanto and its GMO-brethren eventually helped to defeat.

Why? Because Whole Foods has been in bed with Monsanto for a long time, secretly stuffing its shelves with overpriced, fraudulently advertised natural & organic" crap loaded with GMOs, pesticides, rBGH, hormones and antibiotics. So, of course they don't want mandatory labelling as that would expose them as the Whole Frauds and Whore Foods that they really are!

However, when over twenty biotech-friendly companies including [WalMart, Pepsico and ConAgra recently met with FDA](#) in favor of mandatory labelling laws, this after fighting tooth and nail to defeat Prop 37, Whole Foods sees an opportunity to save face and becomes the first grocery chain to announce mandatory labelling of their GMO products...in 2018! Uh, thanks for nothing, Whore.

And if you think its peers have suddenly grown a conscience, think again. They are simply reacting to the public's outcry over the defeat of Prop 37 by crafting deceptive GMO-labelling laws to circumvent any real change, thus keeping the status quo intact.

To add insult to world injury, Monsanto and their partners in crime Archer Daniels Midland, Sodexo and Tyson Foods write and sponsor <u>The Food Safety Modernization Act of 2009: HR 875</u>. This criminal "act" gives the corporate factory farms a virtual monopoly to police and control all foods grown anywhere, including one's own backyard, and provides harsh penalties and jail sentences for those who do not use chemicals and fertilizers. President Obama decided this sounded reasonable and gave his approval.

With this Act, Monsanto claims that only GM foods are safe and organic or homegrown foods potentially spread disease, therefore must be regulated out of existence for the safety of the world. If eating GM pesticide balls is their idea of safe food, I would like to think the rest of the world is smart enough to pass.

As further revelations have broken open regarding this evil giant's true intentions, Monsanto crafted the ridiculous [HR 933 Continuing Resolution, aka Monsanto Protection Act,](#) which Obama robo-signed into law as well. This law states that no matter how harmful Monsanto's GMO crops are and no matter how much devastation they wreak upon the country, U.S. federal courts cannot stop them from continuing to plant them anywhere they choose. Yes, Obama signed a provision that makes Monsanto above any laws and makes them more powerful than the government itself. We have to wonder who's really in charge of the country because it's certainly not him!

There comes a tipping point though when a corporation becomes too evil and the world pushes back...hard! Many countries continue to convict Monsanto of crimes against humanity and have banned them altogether, telling them to "get out and stay out!"

The world has begun to awaken to the fact that the corporate monster does not want control over the global production of food simply for profit's sake. No, it's become clear by over a century of death & destruction that the primary goal is to destroy human health and the environment, turning the world into a Mon-Satanic Hell on Earth!

Research into the name itself reveals it to be latin, meaning "my saint," which may explain why critics often refer to it as "Mon-Satan." Even more conspiratorially interesting is that [free masons and other esoteric societies assigned numbers](#) to each letter in our latin-based alphabet system in a six system. Under that number system, what might Monsanto add up to? Why, of course 6-6-6!

Know that all is not lost. Evil always loses in the end once it is widely exposed to the light of truth as is occurring now. The fact that the Monsanto-led government finds it necessary to enact desperate legislation to protect its true leader proves this point. Being evicted elsewhere, the United States is Monsanto's last stand so to speak.

Yet, even here many have begun striking back by protesting against and rejecting GMO monstrosities, choosing to grow their own foods and shop at local farmers markets instead of the Monsanto-supported corporate grocery chains.

The awakening people are also beginning to see they have been misled by corporate tricksters and federal government criminals poisoned by too much power, control and greed, which has resulted in the creation of the monstrous, out-of-control corporate beast.

NODS

IRT
Institute for Responsible Technology
http://www.responsibletechnology.org/gmo-basics/the-ge-process

Huffington Post Blog
David Kirby
http://www.huffingtonpost.com/david-kirby/food-politics-white-house_b_543798.html

Lenôtre of Paris
http://www.lenotre.com/

GMO Food & Leaky Gut Syndrome
https://hrexach.wordpress.com/2013/09/15/medical-corner-intestinal-permeability-leaky-gut/

Leaky Gut Responsible For MOST Health Issues
http://purenewyou.com/Leaky-Gut-Syndrome.html

Activist Post
http://www.activistpost.com/

The Walking Dead
http://en.wikipedia.org/wiki/The_Walking_Dead_%28TV_series%29

Cancer Facts
http://www.cancerdefeated.com/how-drug-companies-price-what-your-life-is-worth/1266/

Cancer Too Profitable to Allow a Cure! Physicians and the Cancer Factory
http://healthimpactnews.com/2014/the-cancer-industry-is-too-prosperous-to-allow-a-cure/

Whiteout Press
http://www.whiteoutpress.com/articles/q22013/doctors-slam-big-pharma-for-price-gouging-cancer-patients/

Just One Cancer Misdiagnosis Horror Story
(They're are many!)
http://abcnews.go.com/Primetime/story?id=132213

∞

And now . . . a total departure from GMO Foods – with a little something for *Sushi Lovers Everywhere!*

Sushi lover's entire body left riddled with WORMS after eating contaminated sashimi

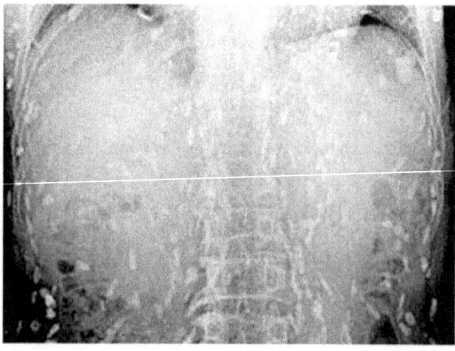

Remember:

<u>You are what you eat!</u>

*Ever wonder
where that saying came from?*

Read on!

∞

"You Are What You Eat"

Meaning

The notion that to be fit and healthy you need to eat good food.

Origin

This phrase has come to us via quite a tortuous route. Anthelme Brillat-Savarin wrote, in *Physiologie du Gout, ou Meditations de Gastronomie Transcendante, 1826*:

"Dis-moi ce que tu manges, je te dirai ce que tu es." [Tell me what you eat and I will tell you what you are].

In an essay titled *Concerning Spiritualism and Materialism*, 1863/4, Ludwig Andreas Feuerbach wrote:

"Der Mensch ist, was er ißt."

That translates into English as 'man is what he eats'.

Neither Brillat-Savarin or Feuerbach meant their quotations to be taken literally. They were stating that that the food one eats has a bearing on what one's state of mind and health.

The actual phrase didn't emerge in English until some time later. In the 1920s and 30s, the nutritionist Victor Lindlahr, who was a strong believer in the idea that food controls health, developed the Catabolic Diet. That view gained some adherents at the time and the earliest known printed example is from an advert for beef in a 1923 edition of the *Bridgeport Telegraph*, for 'United Meet [sic] Markets':

"Ninety per cent of the diseases known to man are caused by cheap foodstuffs. You are what you eat."

In 1942, Lindlahr published *You Are What You Eat: how to win and keep health with diet*. That seems to be the vehicle that took the phrase into the public consciousness. Lindlahr is likely to have also used the term in his radio talks in the late 1930s (now lost unfortunately), which would also have reached a large audience.

The phrase got a new lease of life in the 1960s hippy era. The food of choice of the champions of this notion was macrobiotic wholefood and the phrase was adopted by them as a slogan for healthy eating. The belief in the diet in some quarters was so strong that when Adelle Davis, a leading spokesperson for the organic food movement, contracted the cancer that later killed her, she attributed the illness to the junk food she had eaten at college.

Some commentators have suggested that the idea is from much earlier and that it has a religious rather than dietary basis. Roman Catholics believe that the bread and wine of the Eucharist are changed into the body and blood of Jesus (Transubstantiation).

Is the phrase Catholic rather than catabolic?

Archbishop Thomas Cranmer in 1549:

We offer and present unto thee, O Lord, ourselves, our souls and bodies, to be a reasonable, holy, and living sacrifice unto thee; humbly beseeching thee that we, and all others who shall be partakers of this Holy

Communion, may worthily receive the most precious Body and Blood of thy Son Jesus Christ, be filled with thy grace and heavenly benediction, and made one body with him, that he may dwell in us, and we in him.

Transubstantiation certainly links food and the body, but there doesn't appear to be a clear link between the belief and the phrase. It's safe to assume the origin is more supper than supplication.

∞

Now you know!

The Rest of the Story.

∞

Be sure to catch up on the late, great *–always* innate

Mr. Paul Harvey

and his wonderful segment called:

<u>**The Rest of the Story**</u>

Segments on YouTube:

https://www.youtube.com/results?search_query=the+rest+of+the+story+paul+harvey+playlist

Freedom in 2005

Birth name	Paul Harvey Aurandt
Born	September 4, 1918 Tulsa, Oklahoma, U.S.
Died	February 28, 2009 (aged 90) Phoenix, Arizona, U.S.
Resting place	Forest Home Cemetery, Chicago, Illinois
Alma mater	University of Tulsa
Show	The Rest of the Story Paul Harvey News and Comment
Network	ABC Radio Networks
Country	United States
Spouse(s)	Lynne "Angel" Cooper Harvey (1940–2008; her death)
Children	Paul Harvey, Jr.

Legal Stuff

Any likeness to those living or dead is merely coincidental, *except* where intended.

No part of this publication may be reproduced in whole or in part, or stored in a retrieval system, or transmitted in any form, by any means electronic, mechanical, printing, photocopying, recording, etc. without written consent of the author or publisher, except for the inclusion of brief quotations in a review.

Any art/info used that was obtained from the WWW (World Wide Web) is perceived as part of the Public Domain – used here in accordance with the Fair Use Title

17, U. S. Code Copyright Law. The artists or copyright holders maintain all rights to their creations, and other than our display use of it there is no relationship between us, but we thank them.

For more information, contact the publisher or author.

Google – <u>Golden Panda Publishing</u>

Google – <u>Lyn Murray Writes 2</u>

About the Author

Lyn Murray writes for you – *the reader.*

She is fascinated by anything supernatural, and paranormal. This led her to become the author of **Bane.**

A prolific reader and writer of fiction, Lyn's diverse writing style and mastery of suspense and intrigue is a testament to all those who came before – all the *greats* of long ago that helped shape and mold her technique. In fact – this book is dedicated to them, and if they're watching she hopes they're beaming with pride.

With a politically rich heritage, Lyn is a proud Daughter of the American Revolution; and when she's not playing World of Warcraft with her son, researching natural healing methods, or feeding the ducks on her private lake, she's spinning tales of mysterious what-ifs.

A virtual recluse in her home – <u>Villa Le Paradis Sur Terre</u>, Lyn spends her days researching, reading, writing, and enjoying the simple things in life with her husband over a good cup of coffee and quiet conversation.

Because the back of her Villa is glass from ceiling to floor, Lyn is living proof that people who live in glass houses shouldn't throw stones . . . *they should be writers.*

Lyn's Other Books

Little Book of Memories, Vol. 1
Little Book of Memories, Vol. 2

One Dark Halloween Night

The Howling Man

The Tuck

Nightfall's Day

Glasses Glasses

Paula
[A Nightmare]

The 3rd Sunday of Every Month
[Mystery of White Rose Cemetery]

Who Goes There?
[The Legend of Tally Bottom Ridge]

A Case of Jitters
[Murder at Hammond Hill Rectory]

B.E.K.
[Black Eyed Kid's Phenomenon]

◇◇◇ **and, of course,** ◇◇◇

Blooded
[Anunnaki Rising]

Blooded – Nomads
[Anunnaki Tribulation]

Blooded – Cinder
[Anunnaki Armegeddon]

INDIGENOUS
[Bigfoot People]

Town at the End of Nowhere

BANE

Requiem

. . . with more on the way . . .

◇◇◇

The Wilde Side
Peter Wilde Detective
Lyn's new detective series.

Thank You!

I am honored that you took the time to read my book, and really hope you liked it! If you could, take a moment to let me know what you liked about it. I'd really like to know. Your feedback helps me *hone* my skills.

I'm always looking for new ideas, and developing characters and story plots. Tell me what kind of stories you like – *I write for you!*

See ya' soon.

Bye, bye.

Our Intrepid Duo

Yesterday

Joe age 16

John Tyler High School, Tyler, Texas

Grew up to be a
Chrysler Corporation Executive,
Lee Iacocca Chairman's Award Recipient,
Researcher, Advocate, Activist, Artist, Author,
Poet, and Poker Champ.

Lyn age 16

South Oak Cliff High School
Dallas, Texas

Grew up to be a
Film Processing Industry Executive, Researcher,
Advocate, Activist, Entrepreneur, Artist, Author,
Poet Laureate, and World of Warcraft nerd.

The Salvation Army

Lyn Murray's

BANE

is brought to you

by

Golden Panda Publishing

Read . . .

Just Read!

www.ingramcontent.com/pod-product-compliance
Lightning Source LLC
Chambersburg PA
CBHW051907170526
45168CB00001B/272